Yahya Abbas

FROM BAGHDAD TO TORONTO

A Journey of Values

 FriesenPress

One Printers Way
Altona, MB R0G 0B0
Canada

www.friesenpress.com

ISBN
978-1-03-918511-1 (Hardcover)
978-1-03-918510-4 (Paperback)
978-1-03-918512-8 (eBook)

1. BIOGRAPHY & AUTOBIOGRAPHY, BUSINESS

Distributed to the trade by The Ingram Book Company

DEDICATION

L ife is not a destination but a journey that transcends generations. The stories we write today and ultimately pass on to those who come after us are not the legacy of a single person but the ongoing legacy of the ideas, vision, and values of many people—family.

Like those before me and those who will follow me, this family journey of seven hundred years and counting is not one I have taken alone. While there are many whose lives have positively impacted me, I would like to dedicate this book to two people without whom my journey, my story, and the ending—yet to be written—would not be possible.

As a young boy sitting at a table listening to my father do business, I witnessed firsthand how he lived his values, humility, and integrity every day to the point that it naturally became a part of me. It is to this remarkable man and mentor, Mohammed-Ali Al-Ali, I dedicate my success in business and life that have become the pages of this book I humbly share with you.

Of course, while you will look to those who came before you as mentors, your partners in life provide the encouragement, unwavering support, and enduring belief in you and your dreams that make the journey meaningful. For me, my wife, Nadiea Al-Shami, has not only been my partner but my most trusted confidante and greatest friend. No matter how bright the sun shined or dark the days became, the peace of knowing that she was and would always be at my side enriched me beyond words and measure. To you, with great love, I also dedicate this book.

Prologue:
The Values of Enduring Success

We live in a very complex world, in which new ideas and ideals have replaced familiar and comfortable perceptions. In short, we are in a constant state of change that challenges us to think and do things differently. But is all change good? Does it bring out the best in us or cause us to alter or abandon the core principles of success in the name of expedience or convenience?

A Bump in the Road
Yes, change is inevitable and being able to adapt to new realities is necessary. But what does that adaptation look like, and what does it cost us?

It is often said that you don't really know someone until you hit a bump in the road in which growing pressures requires you to make hard decisions. Your proclaimed values and way of doing business are tested during these difficult times. In other words, it is easy to be a good business partner during good times and not so easy to stay the same course when things go south, testing existing relationships.

Having been successful in the beverage and food manufacturing industry for three decades, I have seen a great deal. I have had to navigate the uncertain waters of shifting and—at times—conflicting interests. One example of a relationship disconnect is the recent news that one of Canada's biggest food manufacturers is no longer shipping its products to the country's largest grocer. The point of contention is the manufacturers' efforts to recoup higher costs brought about by both the pandemic and emerging geopolitical issues. The grocer believes that the manufacturer is trying to use inflation as a reason to justify unreasonable price hikes.

Conversely, the manufacturer believes that the grocer is using their market strength to bully the supplier and pad their bottom line. It is clear that there is a trust issue in which contention and mistrust have replaced collaboration and cooperation. By the way, situations such as these are not confined to the food industry.

While I make no judgements regarding the desire to achieve a healthy bottom line, I cannot help but wonder if the seeds for discontent were sown long before the crisis period we are now in came about.

The Values of Enduring Success

As a manufacturer and businessman, I understand the points of contention in the above example. I also understand why the relationship between the two has come to a loggerhead. The question isn't whether or not either party's concerns are legitimate—they are. The issue is the approach taken to address said concerns, in which the situation calls for transparency and trust versus assuming an adversarial stance.

Once again, I am not judging the parties' actions. Having said that, getting beyond impasses such as this one is something with which I have had experience and success.

The secret of my success during both good and challenging times isn't really a secret—it all comes down to values. That is the focus of this book: what the values of enduring success are.

In sharing my family's generational journey from Baghdad to Toronto with you, I hope to provide you with more than a story—although it is a good story. My intention with writing this book is not only to entertain and engage you. I want to challenge you to perhaps see the world differently, including how you do business.

While it is indeed a brave and—at times—complex new world, the values that define your approach to business and your ultimate success are timeless and unchanging.

What makes this book different is that I am not simply going to provide you with a business to-do list. I will take it a step further by showing you the direct link between my approach and the tangible and enduring success my companies have achieved, spanning the many decades I have been in business.

"What we do for ourselves dies with us. What we do for others and the world remains and is immortal." – Albert Pike

CHAPTER 1:
Seven Hundred Years of Values

*"The way to transform your immense inner value into outer riches is
by giving it freely and authentically to others." – Ralph Marston*

While I am reluctant to make broad statements about
any group of people or society in general, I remember
reading that generosity and humility are at the top
of the list of the many values that are honoured in Iraqi culture.
Again, while I cannot speak for everyone, I can confidently tell you
that these were the core values or principles by which my father
ran our textile company – the largest textile business in Iraq.

As I reflect on those years sitting at a table as a young boy,
listening to my father do business, I witnessed firsthand the link
between personal values and success. In other words, I was a
firsthand witness to how my father lived his values, humility, and
integrity every day, to the point that it naturally became a part
of me.

Now, I think that this is an important point to make, because the prevailing attitude in business—especially during difficult times such as we are experiencing today—is a zero-sum approach in which one can only win at the expense of another. When you do business in this manner, there is little transparency, as each player seeks to manipulate the situation to their advantage rather than collaborate. While this approach may bring about a short-term gain, it usually comes at a far greater cost over the mid to long term. How you do business reflects you and your personal values. The only way to turn your "immense inner value into outer riches" is, as Ralph Marston says, "by giving it freely and authentically to others."

Seven Hundred Years
In this context, our family's inner value reflected our way of giving freely and authentically to others through our businesses. Interestingly, while my father was the one who set an example for me on the way to conduct business and life, this mindset did not originate with him when he started his textile business in 1956. It started more than seven hundred years ago with our family's first textile business. That's right; our family had been in the textile business for seven hundred years when my father began his company in the 1950s.

Undoubtedly, the experience gained over several generations gave us a high level of expertise in the textile industry. One might look at that and say that was our competitive advantage. However, as valuable as intimate knowledge of a particular business or industry may be, and it is an important factor, our sustaining success over so many centuries had as much to do with how we did business versus what business we did.

I am saying that the way we did business would have produced the same results in any industry. The fact that I have been very successful in the rattan furniture and various food industries, as my children have been in their respective business ventures, gives testimony to this fact.

Unlike specific job skills or capabilities, the values that drive your enduring success are transferable to any field or job. I say transferable because you can acquire expertise or learn how to do something, but the values by which you do business are an intrinsic part of who you are and what you believe. For example, when I came to Canada, I went into the rattan furniture and gift basket business. I had no previous experience in this field, but I dedicated the time to learning everything I could about it. While learning the technical requirements of a job is essential, I believe that my ultimate success was how I did business. Over the years, I have heard from many individuals that I am the most trusted person in the industry because people see it. Truth and how you conduct yourself in business relations becomes your personal brand. They call it personal branding now; I call it personal integrity.

Do not get me wrong, acquiring the right skills to do the best job is vital, as is innovative thinking—how you can make a business's products and serve customers better. We will talk more about this in the upcoming chapters. That said, your success all starts with the personal brand you create through open and honest dealings with those both within and external to your company. Truth is truth!

A Valuable Lesson

Trust and transparency are the key tenets of doing business, especially during tough economic times. You need to always work with people you trust.

For a year after dad acquired the beverage business, he asked me to work with the previous owner to help me transition from his ownership to mine. He was a seventy-one-year-old gentleman and, as I would soon discover, was crooked.

During this time, I learned all the ways people play the game and cheat. There are a lot of lies in the business world. However, as unpleasant as it was to work with this fellow, he still taught me an important lesson. Because he showed me how crooked business was done, I could more readily spot dishonesty in other people from that day forward.

Honesty between partners and in how they conduct themselves in their dealings speaks volumes. If you know what to look for, you will work with likeminded people, honest people whose values will align with your values. That is why if you are honest—especially when it is most difficult, people will take a chance to help you and support you and vice versa. In other words, choose your partners wisely—and when I say partners, I am talking about employees, suppliers and, yes, customers.

You cannot have a mutually profitable relationship when the other person or persons you are dealing with are not honest. All you are doing is giving yourself a headache in which the supposed benefits of the relationship—e.g., building a successful enterprise and making money for all involved—will never warrant your investment of time or energy.

Recognizing Honesty

While I can spot a dishonest partner because I know the right way to do business, it is also easier to recognize honesty in people.

How do I know that they are honest?

One example that has stayed with me my entire life was when my father lowered his prices when a recession hit in the 1970s and paid back his customers the price difference. He did it so that his customers would not lose money and could afford to do business during tough economic times. Like all difficult times, the recession would end, and people would not go to his competitors—only to him, because of what he did. By the way, he still made money when many other companies were struggling, eventually ending up with 55 percent of the market share.

Many years later, I was similarly proactive with one of the country's largest grocery chains. They saw me as a trusted partner, and it was well known that people would not lose money with me. As a result, there was full transparency in our relationship. Because we could be transparent, we were able to negotiate our prices during a tough economy that were mutually beneficial.

Ironically, they didn't share the same level of trust with another supplier and pulled that company's products from their shelves. Similar to my father in the 1970s, I made money while so many businesses could not make ends meet.

As I said earlier, when you are honest, people are willing to take a chance with you and support you.

A memorable example of how people will work with you if you are honest comes from a businessman I met in 2017 in Melbourne, Australia.

As he was launching a new retail business, he had limited funding. Needing a location for his enterprise, he came across the perfect building. Unfortunately, the four-dollar cost per square foot was well over his budget. However, because he was open with the building's owner about his vision for the business and his current finances, the owner rented the facility to him at $1.50 a square foot. As part of their agreement, the property owner said that as his business grew and became successful, he would raise the rate accordingly. Well, the business grew, and he ended up paying the agreed price increase. The business was so successful that he even built an addition to the building, which enabled the owner to make even more money.

Everybody Wins

Beyond being straightforward in your dealings with people, I will talk about the importance of not betting more you can lose on a business venture in the upcoming chapters. I will also discuss the importance of investing the time and energy to learn everything about your business and the market you are looking to serve.

In the meantime, the point of this first chapter is honesty and how it is a talent that is readily available to everyone who wants it. Everyone can have integrity, which makes success accessible to everyone—because people are not blind, nor are they dumb. They can recognize integrity, honesty, and solid values.

Whether you own a business or are an employee being honest in the way you do your job—be it as a CEO or frontline employee—is the not-so-secret secret for a successful life.

For example, late one Friday evening, an employee called me at home—yes, I was always accessible to my employees, encouraging them to speak their minds and share any concerns with me. In this case, the individual shared with me two offers of employment he had received in which he would earn 30 percent above the going market rate. He asked me what I thought.

I told him that people are always willing to pay more for something when there is a desperate need. The market was booming, and skilled, proven employees were hard to come by. As long as the need persisted, offers like the ones he showed me would continue. However, based on my experience in the industry, when the market takes its inevitable shift in the other direction, the first people companies will lay off are the ones who have the highest salaries. In other words, the urgent needs will pass—and your value to them with it.

Market conditions should not determine your long-term value because the market constantly changes. Your value—your real value, I told him—is based on the integrity of your work and your willingness to do more than what is asked of you.

Now, I know what you may be thinking: I said what I did because I did not want to give him a raise. But ask yourself this question: why did this employee call me at home and ask to meet me over the weekend? Why, already having not one but two great offers in hand, would he not just accept one of them and move on? What would you do if you were in his shoes and worked for a boss you didn't trust or respect?

As you have been reading through the pages of this book, you have seen that I have always striven to give my clients the best of the best in product quality at a fair price. This commitment to my customers isn't one-way. I have that same attitude toward those I work with and the many people who work for me.

While I would never discount the importance of the financial aspect of business, I also understand that money will only go so far, and that it alone does not bring lasting satisfaction or fulfill a sustainable sense of purpose. No different than me, dedicated and successful people want to feel like they are a part of something special and are making a difference. If I were only interested in getting someone for the lowest salary, what kind of people do you think I would attract to work for me? Conversely, if I only looked to hire people whose primary or sole goal was to make as much money as possible, what impact would that have on the quality of their work and loyalty to the company's vision to deliver the highest quality for a fair price? This last point is what I mean when I use the term "integrity of work."

By the way, the employee came to me a couple of years later and thanked me for the advice I had given him that weekend, and told me that he was glad that he stayed with me, because he was now the company's national manager.

CHAPTER 2:
Rattan to Popcorn

"The secret of success is constancy of purpose." – Benjamin Disraeli

I doubt that anyone would disagree with me when I say that we live in an increasingly complicated world in which there is great change and much uncertainty. In business terms, it is known as VUCA—which refers to the volatility, uncertainty, complexity, and ambiguity we all, to varying degrees, face on a daily basis.

According to the Niagara Institute, during times of uncertainty, business leaders need an ability to "shift and respond to changes in the business environment with corresponding actions that are focused, quick, and agile." In other words, we have to be ready to change direction quickly and effectively to meet the demands of a market that seems to be in a state of perpetual transition.

However, what is interesting is that being responsive to changing market conditions also requires a high level of consistency when it comes to your values or a sense of purpose. In short, what is your purpose for being in business? Why do you do what you do? What motivates you to go into work each day, and what are you prepared to do to make your vision and values a reality?

Regardless of the products or services you provide, knowing the answer to these questions is the foundation on which you will build enduring success.

Rattan to Popcorn

Whether manufacturing rattan furniture and gift baskets, introducing the country's first microwave popcorn, first Pringles chip knock-off, and first aseptic PET production using a dry system in Canada, my success over the past thirty-seven years is the result of knowing my purpose for being in business.

What was—and is—my purpose? Delivering a high-quality product at a fair price, on time—all of the time.

Let's look at my first business in Canada. When I was in my mid-twenties, Dad purchased a rattan furniture and gift basket business for me. It was December 1985.

During the transition period, I worked closely with the previous owner and grew the business by 20 percent in the first year. Not long afterwards, I was able to land a $750,000 order for patio furniture with the country's largest retailer at the time (Eaton's), which was a dollar amount that was unheard of back then. A short time later, I landed a second notable contract with another major retail chain—Towers. While not as big as the previous deal with Eaton's, it solidified my company's position as the top rattan furniture supplier.

Our line of wicker gift baskets was also a hit, as chains such as Body Shop used our baskets to showcase their premium bath supply products, while florists used what we made as decorative planters for flowers.

Now, you might think, *patio furniture and gift baskets?* How do you differentiate what many consider to be ubiquitous products?

The answer is simple: I saw a different way to do the business that elevated the quality of the product to an entirely new level on a cost-effective basis.

It should come as no surprise that this was the formula I used to build successful enterprises in the juice and—later—snack business (remember my earlier reference to microwave popcorn).

So, how did I elevate the quality of the product in the rattan business? I owned a small paint shop and turned it into a production facility to paint the gift baskets and rattan furniture. Of course, it wasn't just a simple process of slapping on a few coats of paint that made our products very attractive to the consumer. It was making a quality product that was affordable for the masses.

Commoditizing Quality
As I said, the quality of our products made a difference.

Let's consider our line of rattan patio furniture, which I purchased semi-finished from China, and which always sold out very fast.

Your first question is likely, *why didn't the competition purchase the same furniture from China that you did?* I don't know; maybe they did. What they didn't do was make a better product—both in looks and durability.

We employed a four-step process with our automated paint booth that no one else did. First, we would prepare the furniture's surface by burning or scorching it to remove the shvires of the rattan. We did this because it created a surface that would better absorb the initial coat of water-based paint and give it a cleaner look. We would then add two coats of oil-based paint, making the color pop and protecting the furniture from the elements. Because our process improved durability, the furniture maintained its store-bought look over time. Once again, we were a successful company because of my unwavering commitment to always to find a better way to deliver a great quality product at a fair price.

The Origins of Purpose

As I said, a big differentiator for our rattan business was our process to make our products stand out, including the use of high-quality paint. In this regard, we did what our competitors were unwilling to do, which was to always look for a cost-effective way to deliver a superior product.

Note that I said *unwilling*, not *unable*, to do it. To this day and given our then-market share, I do not understand why our competitors didn't elevate their game to build a quality brand at competitive pricing.

What was their purpose for being in business? If you can't do something better than anyone else, why do it? Why buy a company that you can't improve or take in new and exciting directions?

Growing up in Baghdad, I loved working with mechanical devices and wood-finishing when I was a kid. In the context of the rattan business, my mechanical interests enabled me to convert a paint shop into a production shop on a cost-effective basis. As for wood finishing, it taught me everything I needed to know about creating a quality product, e.g., our four-step process of scorching and painting the furniture we brought in from China.

I also had a good eye for how a product would or could look, as I had an artistic sense that—with my father's encouragement—I developed between Grades 7 and 10. During that time, I produced geographic maps and various forms of art through which I gained a good deal of recognition. Of course, I loved doing it, as it was not only a talent but a passion.

Working with the family in the factory also gave me knowledge beyond the functional elements of a business. One lesson I learned is that taking a common-sense approach to any business, in which you continuously look for a better way to do something that no one else is doing, works for any product or service you are selling. For me, this was the origin of my purpose—to do or make something better.

Having Common Sense

In the previous section, I referred to the importance of taking a common-sense approach to business.

Beyond finding a better way to do something, having common sense also means you should never look at a business from a money-only standpoint. If you do, you are working from a position of weakness, having to make a sale. You want to work from a position of strength in which you do not have the financial burden of *I need this* versus *I want to do this*. As I said earlier, I never made an investment in which I could not afford to lose the said investment.

For example, let's look at the big Eaton's order for a thousand patio sets. I am not exaggerating when I said that we came out of nowhere to land what was, at the time, the industry's biggest order.

The business with Eaton's was an important sale in my life because I did what my competitors at the time would never do—find a way to deliver a superior product at a fair price in which everyone, on all sides of the deal, made money. I am not just talking about win-win but having a *win-win mindset*.

What is a "win-win" mindset?

Suppose your primary objective is to make as much money as you can. In that case, you will not necessarily do everything you should to get to a real win-win relationship with your suppliers and end customers. Think about it for a moment: why didn't my competitors come up with a four-step scorch-and-paint process? After winning big contracts with major retailers, why didn't they start developing their version of my process to enable them to deliver a great product on time and at a fair price?

I suspect that they didn't because their focus or purpose was to make as much money as possible. Adding extra steps to scorch and paint the products would increase their costs and cut into profits. While I was not privy to their financial situation, I do know that the business I did was not only more sizeable but profitable as well.

Do not get me wrong; I was never in business to lose money. However, rather than looking for better margins, I looked for ways to make a better product. I don't think you can do that if money is your primary objective.

Wicker to Juice

From a people and revenue standpoint, over the three years I owned the rattan company, I was able to double the size of the business. Taking over a business that had been in existence for twenty years before me buying it, doubling it in size, and expanding it into a notable industry brand was quite an accomplishment. I needed new challenges.

So, when my father decided to buy a juice business, I saw it as an opportunity to make a change—especially since I knew that I could enjoy even greater success by bringing the same sense of purpose to it. After all, the market size for juice products was considerably larger than the rattan business. And, as mentioned at the beginning of the chapter, I could see even more ways to make the juice business better.

You may be wondering what happened to the rattan business. I sold it to someone who, in turn, eventually sold it to another player in the market.

Know Your Purpose

Unlike the rattan business—which was in existence for twenty years before I took over, the juice business we purchased was a failing division of a larger company that had only been around for about a year.

When I eventually sold it, eight years later, it was the largest juice manufacturer in Canada and the Northeastern United States. How did I get there?

Selecting the right business in the right market at the right time is another contributing factor to my success—be it rattan furniture, juice, or snacks.

Before buying any business, the deciding question to answer for me is whether I could make it better. In short, if I can't, I won't buy it.

As previously indicated, the juice company was a relatively new business that had started up the previous year. The owner—who I would later discover was a crook—had opened many juice companies around the world. (By the way, the former owner of the juice company could be the subject for a second book. But that is also a story for another day.)

Losing two million dollars a year, the owner cooked the books to show it as profitable. He eventually went bankrupt. Despite this, we went ahead with the purchase, confident that we could turn it into a winning company. After all, the product was good and the market was wide open.

Once again, over the eight years I ran the juice business, I was able to build it into a major success.

As with my previous rattan enterprise, I did this by leveraging technology to reduce production costs while delivering a high-quality product on time and at an affordable price. We will talk more about the juice business in an upcoming chapter. In the meantime, the underlying message from this chapter is knowing your purpose for getting into any business.

What about the popcorn?

In the next chapter, we will talk about the snack business—which is also my current business.

CHAPTER 3:
An Eye-Popping Opportunity

After selling the juice business, I knew I wanted to get into the snack business, simply because I liked it—the products were cool.

I had many good friends through my network of people—including friendly competitors like Cott Beverages' president, Mark Benadiba.

At that time, Cott had purchased Murphy's Potato Chips from Galen Weston's wife and her brother—who was a Murphy.

Because the Murphy chip business was struggling, Galen Weston Sr. sold the company to Cott.

Cott was not doing well with it either, so I asked Mark if he would sell me the Murphy business. He told me it wasn't a good business and he didn't want to sell it to me. He told me, instead, that a company called Super-Pufft was on the market. I met with the owner of Super-Pufft—Doug, a former Loblaws employee. Super-Pufft, which opened in 1946, was losing money when I decided to buy it. Sadly, everything they had for production technology was antiquated. But they had two accounts that were of interest to me—one was Loblaws and the other was A&P.

I could see the possibilities with these two clients because I had connections in the industry, and I could definitely make the business better by building an entirely new plant in Concord, Ontario. I bought Super-Pufft in 1995 and moved to our new manufacturing facility in Concord in 1996.

One of the first things I did was to put in high-speed caramel corn and filling machines in a new space, with new visibility, at the new plant. I scrapped everything but the packaging from the old plant, which, with its other flaws, had an infestation of cockroaches. There was no way I would take the risk of using anything from that facility. I then started doing business with Sobey's, John Vince, and the Skydome through McDonald's.

A couple of years later, in 1997, I landed Kernels, supplying them with corn, oil, and other products—which was a sizeable business win. We were doing well with popcorn.

A New Chip in the Game

In late 1997, I was having lunch with Dale McDonald, the vice president of Oshawa Foods, and he told me that he hated it when someone came in and said to him that they were raising the price for a bag of chips by five cents a unit. I said, "give me your business, and I will do it for you—give me a five-year contract." He offered three years. I insisted on five years.

While we took time to think about the Oshawa opportunity, I wondered if the same thing was happening with other retail chains. Within the next few days, I approached Loblaws and told them I wanted to get into the chip business and know what they needed. Beyond delivering a quality product comparable to the national brand, Loblaws wanted a longer shelf life and competitive pricing.

Once again, the need was to provide quality products at a fair price. It was something the competitors were not willing to do because, as I was told, "they were arrogantly confident that they could do what they wanted." Loblaws was interested!

I knew I had to upgrade our lines further to meet the new chip demand.

I had an IT guy that had worked for me in the past who had two buddies who designed a system for CP Rail that enabled operator-free train movement in the trainyard back and forth. I knew I had to meet with them. The result was that they ultimately designed a concept that automated the entire chip manufacturing process from the start of production to the delivery of the chips. What was exciting was that the product was handled only once. The new process meant that the chips got to Loblaws right off the production line—a just-in-time approach mirroring auto industry production techniques for potato chips instead of cars.

We also filled the bag with nitrogen to remove both the moisture and the air to ensure minimal breakage and extended freshness of the chips in the bag, for eight to ten weeks. Also, as mentioned previously, our one-touch manufacturing process—the industry average for touches was ten times greater—meant that we could consistently deliver a quality product. After all, the more you handle a product, the greater the risk for chip breakage.

I went to Loblaws and said we could deliver the quality chip product they required at a better price than what they were paying to their current supplier. I then asked them for a commitment to buy thirty tonnes a week for five years, with the understanding that we would deliver our product no more than five days after leaving our plant. They gave me a letter confirming the terms, and we were now in the chip and popcorn businesses.

We then set up a state-of-the-art manufacturing plant in Mississauga to produce up to eighty tonnes per week—or two thousand pounds an hour. We could meet Loblaws production requirements in a single day through the new facility.

While production speed was important, maintaining the highest level of quality and taste was vital.

Once again, offering a quality product at a fair price using an innovative approach to manufacturing is the winning formula, regardless of what you are selling.

Back To Popcorn

I relocated the popcorn business from Concord to Mississauga because the latter was bigger and newer.

Serving the market through concessions, e.g., McDonald's at the Skydome and the more than eighty Kernels locations across Canada, and the retail grocery chains, we offered popcorn and chips.

What was our next innovation? Obviously, microwave popcorn.

When I entered this market, no one made the product in Canada. It was made in the US and shipped to Canada. So, we put in the line to make microwave popcorn for international and domestic customers, including small Canadian retailers, filling a notable gap in the market that our competitors didn't serve. We also had a significant market share in Mexico, a country that more readily embraced the new product. In short, we were the only company in Canada to manufacture microwave popcorn.

The smaller retailers were one segment of the market that loved the convenience and quality of the product because it provided great taste at a reasonable price for everyone, right through to the consumer.

However, after two and a half years, I moved the product's manufacturing to Mexico to better serve that burgeoning market and free up manufacturing capacity for our popular core products back home. As a businessman, I had the foresight to get into the domestic microwave popcorn business, and loved it. However, you have to align your product strategy and manufacturing capacity to meet the demands of the markets you are serving. When that alignment didn't happen here in Canada, I was willing to change course.

In other words, just because you love the idea or—in this case—the product you are selling, doesn't mean that you should ignore reality. The Mexican market for microwave popcorn was significant and growing faster than the Canadian market. In the meantime, the demand for our other products—traditional popcorn and potato chips—was growing significantly here at home, requiring an increase in the output capacity of our Mississauga facility. Given this reality, it was the best decision for everyone.

You can love your product, but you have to love the market you are serving more.

The Walmart Story

Have you ever seen the packaging for Fuji water?

As a food industry manufacturer, I was fascinated with the product name and its packaging—I loved everything about it.

I loved it so much that I actually considered going into business with the Vancouver-based company, renting space in my Mississauga facility for warehousing the water.

However, in another example of the importance of loving the market more than a product, they relocated their business back to Vancouver when they couldn't gain meaningful traction with consumers. I, of course, didn't pursue the opportunity to get into the water business.

Although the Fuji water opportunity didn't materialize, it did give me a great idea when an opportunity with the world's top retailer, Walmart, presented itself. In 2020, Walmart generated $559 billion in revenue. This staggering total was more than the combined earnings of the four other companies that made up the top-five list. I am talking about companies such as Costco and Amazon.

Like Water for Pringles

As I said earlier, I was really impressed with the creativity behind the packaging of Fuji water—I loved everything about it. So, when the sales representative (Steve), who I met through the water company, told me that Walmart was looking for a canister chip, a Pringles knock-off, the wheels began to turn.

Like Fuji water, where the packaging and the product quality were top-notch, I knew I could do something similar for a no-name-brand, Pringles-style potato chip by bringing together innovative packaging with a high-quality product inside at a fair price. Remember, that is my formula for success.

Steve asked me if I could do it, and when I told him yes, he made an appointment to meet with a senior executive at Walmart.

Three days later, I entered the office of the senior vice president, Bob Anderson, in the United States with a sample can. Before meeting with Bob, I had an artist design a new label for a sleeve that I put over a Pringles can to create the sample can for the new chip. You have to remember, at this stage, the non-branded version of Pringles was a concept more than a reality. But it was a concept that I was confident I could pull off based on my experience with transforming the rattan and juice businesses.

You should note that I also brought actual food samples of our popcorn and potato chips to demonstrate that we could deliver a high-quality product.

We sat down in the meeting room with Bob Anderson and the Walmart team and presented our samples. At that point, Bob said that they had previously met with five other companies about this project, but none had brought with them any samples. So, because I brought a sample can, I won the business.

I then said I needed a five-year agreement.

Bob told me, "We don't do that."

I said, "If I am going to spend five million dollars to get this product produced, I need to have a solid agreement."

He again said, "we do not do this," e.g., enter into an agreement.

I said, "Come on, Bob, we are spending five million dollars on the new line."

He said, yet again, "We don't do that."

I said, "Look, we dealt with your counterpart in Canada on a promotion where they committed to a certain volume and only bought 10 percent of what was promised."

Bob got up and left the office. I didn't know why he left, but he returned with five people from the reception area a short time later. In front of me, Bob asked them how long they had been doing business with Walmart as a supplier. Ten years was the response.

"Have we ever screwed you?"

"No, you haven't."

He repeated this process four or five times, with all suppliers offering the same response. I looked at Bob and said, "I got the message, no problem, we will do it without a contract."

He said, "You have the business."

I then gave him an estimated cost of around fifty-six cents per unit. He said, "I will take it." The estimated volume was a hundred million units.

Before we left, I said to Bob, "We do a line of potato chips as well." He said, "I'm not interested." I said, "Just try it; what do you have to lose?"

I opened the no-name bag of chips I made for Loblaws. I used the Loblaws product because Walmart admires Loblaws products. I had never seen a bag of chips like this. They were golden in colour, with not a single broken chip, with an incredible, mature taste. They were the perfect chips.

He looked at it and said, "I want some samples."

I told him, "I don't give samples."

He then picked up the phone and said, "Dan, you have to come down here and see something."

When Dan arrived, Bob told him to look in the bag, after which Dan said, "Send us some samples."

Looking over to Bob, I said, "I don't send samples."

Bob said, "I need to know your price."

I said, "Thirty-eight and a half cents."

He said, "The business is yours; send me samples."

Bob then looked at the big bag of chips and said, "What about the big bag?"

I said it cost $1.15 or $1.12.

He said, "Come back with samples for that."

Walmart not only purchased the no-name Pringles-style product, but also our line of bagged chips.

What about the popcorn?

They added our popcorn line to the deal at the next meeting. Three product lines in all: a Pringles version of chips, bagged chips, and popcorn.

Within eighteen months, we achieved an annual run rate with Walmart of twenty-eight million dollars.

The Right Number of Crunches

Landing a major deal as I did with Walmart is one thing. Delivering on it is another.

As part of our R&D process, I flew to Italy to check out the machine that would be able to produce the Pringles-type chip. I worked with the R&D people to mimic the Pringles product.

Many people do not know what is involved with making such a chip. You need to ensure that the person eating the chip gets eighteen or nineteen crunches per chip.

After multiple tries, we finally did it—we successfully made our version of the Pringles chip.

As an interesting aside, the Italian company I was dealing with also dealt with Pepsi, who wanted to get into the Pringle's knock-off business. The difference is that they tried to use plastic containers.

Now, you may be wondering at this point, *why eighteen to nineteen crunches?* Because the crunch is like music to the consumer's ear—they want great taste, and they want the crunch.

We were selling not only taste but a taste experience. People who really understand our business know what makes a product different from a competitor's goes beyond name brand and packaging. The first is the crunch, then the flavour, shape, etc. If you meet all of these criteria, you will have a successful product.

An Unexpected Twist

After confirming that I could produce the final product, I returned to visit Walmart in Arkansas.

They asked me if I had secured my can supply for the chips during that meeting. I said yes, I had secured the supply with a company, Sonoco.

Walmart asked me to get a letter from them confirming it. On my drive back to the airport—it was a Thursday, I called and asked Glenn, the Sonoco sales representative, if he could get me a letter confirming the supply of their cans. He assured me that getting a letter would not be a problem.

The following day on Friday, at 7 a.m., I received a call from Glenn telling me that he had talked with his boss and they could not guarantee their supply.

I said, "Glenn, I just laid down five million dollars to build the line. Why are you telling me this now? Why didn't you tell me in the beginning?!"

Glenn said it wasn't up to him; it was his boss. So, I asked for his boss's phone number and then called him. The boss was a really bad guy—the worst salesperson you could ever meet—no sympathy on his part, just a screw-you attitude.

Despite promising to think it over, the boss never got back to me.

I needed to find an alternative source for the cans.

I found another can manufacturer in Germany through a contact in the United States (Stone Containers). However, Stone Containers said that they could work with us to make the cans, including building the lines, as their interest was in the paper for the labels.

I called the German company and talked to the sales guy, who said that the cost of making our own cans using our paper was eight to nine cents. If we bought a finished can from them, with labels, our cost would be sixteen and a half cents, plus freight, for a total cost per unit of twenty cents. That number didn't work.

After thinking about it, I called the German company back and asked if they had a line built so I could manufacture our own cans. They said yes, they had a line available and were going to showcase it at an exhibition in May in Germany. I flew out to Germany in May, went to the exhibition, and bought the line. That was a Sunday.

On Monday, I flew back to Toronto, and on Tuesday morning, I got a call from Sonoco. They said they had heard I had bought the line to build the cans. I said yes, but that I wanted them to tell their boss that he had made a mistake and I would not forget. I am sure I will get back at him and cost him a lot of profit. Also, show him that a little guy like me is powerful.

You may be wondering why Sonoco would burn a bridge with me.

I found out later that Procter & Gamble (P&G) buys a million cans from Sonoco, and P&G, who happened to sell Pringles, told them they would cut them off if they supplied me with the cans.

By the way, P&G eventually sold the Pringles brand to Kellogg's in 2012.

Despite Sonoco's (and P&G's) efforts to derail our business with Walmart, I found a better way to deliver our product at a better cost. It is safe to say that Sonoco underestimated my resolve to get it done, as they believed I did not have the experience to find an alternative source.

In hindsight, they would have been wiser to help me fulfill the first orders for Walmart and then pull the rug out from under me. It certainly would have created a more challenging situation for me. However, doing what they did when they did it allowed me not only to find an alternative solution for the Pringles-type container. My ingenuity in solving the problem led to my business with Walmart growing from twenty-eight million dollars to forty and then fifty million per year.

How did that happen?

It started with Walmart ordering one million cases of juice boxes from me.

CHAPTER 4:
Back to the Future

A s stated in an earlier chapter, when I sold my first juice business, it was to someone I thought shared my values and business approach in terms of running a company from the standpoint of serving the market versus solely themselves.

Ultimately (and unfortunately), they went their own way, seeking higher profits than one could reasonably expect for the business they were running. In other words, they priced themselves out of the market and would end up declaring bankruptcy. Of course, that is another story for another book.

Now that they were gone, they had customers who were left hanging. One of them—a wholesaler with over a thousand stores, such as IGA, Food City, and Dutch Boy—needed a new (and reliable) source. Their request that I start a new company to support their significant demand was a determining factor in my decision to get back into the juice business.

Who was the wholesaler? Oshawa Foods. That's right; I am talking about the same Oshawa Foods with whom I could not reach an agreement to provide them with chips. As a sidenote, Oshawa Foods eventually added my line of chips to their store shelves to complement my popcorn product, which they had been selling for some time. I will talk about this in the chapter on over-coming obstacles—including how not to burn bridges.

Now, and as in the past, my proven formula in which I would take an existing product and find a better way to produce a higher-quality alternative at a lower price point was the basis for my success with this latest enterprise. It is no small irony that the product I was replacing in this instance was one of my own, from the now-defunct juice company.

Since I already had the manufacturing infrastructure through my snack business, expanding into the juice business was straight-forward, because I wasn't entering a new market but returning to an old, familiar one. My setup streamlined my re-entry into the market, in which companies such as Walmart and Coca-Cola were also customers. It also enabled me to use our state-of-the-art facilities to produce a better final product.

A Little Help from My Friends

Having a good understanding of the juice market meant that I had a clear vision of what I had to do to make it happen, but it also meant that I could avoid some of the potential obstacles experienced by a new enterprise.

I do not want to give you the false impression that there weren't a few twists and turns along the way. As a business owner, the line between starting a business and achieving success is often not a straight line.

I shifted product lines at my manufacturing facility to meet Oshawa's immediate demand. I could do this because my relation-ship with another client, Coca-Cola, enabled me to ask them if I could cut back on their Minute Maid delivery needs for a short period to meet the production requirements of Oshawa Foods.

You will need a little help from your friends every now and then, which is a two-way street, as you will find out later in this chapter.

Of course, once my production lines were set up to meet the Oshawa demand, I was able to resume normal production levels for Coca-Cola.

Now, you may be wondering why I was able to win Oshawa's juice business when we couldn't initially get them to work with us on the chip deal. I think it was Louis Pasteur who said something along the lines of chance favoring the prepared mind. As I look back, many successes were the result of timing and being ready to step forward to say yes with confidence when an opportunity presented itself. My timing always seemed good, because I was always prepared for success through my commitment to always find a better way to deliver a product at a fair price while still being profitable in the process.

With chips, the timing wasn't right for Oshawa; with juice, it was not only the right time, but it was also the *only* time, as they had an immediate, urgent need. By the way, Oshawa did sign a contract for juice.

I don't know how I did it when faced with such an urgent request, but I can confidently say that no one else could have done what I did. Regardless of the product I was making, my reputation as an innovator and problem-solver has served me well throughout my entire business career.

Oshawa Foods had a history with me in my snack business— popcorn—and they were my first customer with my earlier juice business. It is also worth noting that another former customer, Loblaws, had a similar problem when the owner of my former juice company went bankrupt and left them hanging—though, unlike Oshawa, they did have other juice suppliers. Because I was a proven partner over the years, they became customers of my new juice business, as did Walmart.

Reliability and Partnership—It's the Real Thing

Today, our snack and juice companies are the largest manufacturer in our market in Canada and the largest in the Northeastern United States.

Outside of the big chains, including A&P, Oshawa Foods, Walmart Canada, and Coca-Cola, we also service smaller retail chains in the United States.

We produce the Minute Maid brand for the big bottler in our relationship with Coca-Cola. Coke has worked with me for many years, because we deliver a great quality product at a good price, never having an issue with timely delivery. In the process—and not just with Coke, but with all of our clients, we are the behind-the-scenes manufacturing partner for the brands we serve. What this means is that if any of our customers sell a major brand for which we do the manufacturing process (remember how P&G sold the Pringles brand to Kellogg's), we are part of the brand package that the buying company acquires. In other words, we are part of their value proposition for the brand, because we provide out-of-the-gate, turnkey manufacturing support that is 100 percent reliable.

This last point is important because the process of changing manufacturing companies is significant, taking between eighteen to twenty-four months or longer to set up a line.

The question is, "What are they going to change through a different manufacturing arrangement?"

In the past thirty-four years of serving Coca-Cola, there was never a problem once their product left our factory. We are a trusted partner.

In fact, they never visit our plants, because they have never experienced a problem with us. We bring an innovative and mechanical view of things that transcends specific industries, as demonstrated by my success with earlier businesses, from scorching the patio furniture for Eaton's to the no-name Pringles packaging and product we developed for Walmart. With us, innovation is not a one-time thing. We are not just a passthrough manufacturer offering little more than the lines we set up to meet our customers' needs. We are an innovative partner, and we take a great deal of pride in becoming an integral part of the brand offering. That is the difference between a transaction-driven business relationship and "partnership."

Partnering or Pricing

A big company with whom have done a great deal of business over the years recently asked one of our sales representatives if we could produce and deliver a new vegetable product for them. As always, I was up for the challenge, and said no problem.

However, when we reviewed the contract with a member of their procurement team, there was a clause indicating that we had to match any price quote they received from a competitor during the life of the contract. I said either we are a partner with you or nothing. In other words, because we are not a transactional company but a strategic partner, having to match low-ball bids from companies who do not have the same expertise or track record that we have built up over the years is unacceptable. You need to decide: do you want a partner in this new venture, or do you want to limit your relationship to the lowest bidder?

They removed the clause.

Beyond a Single Line

From a single line to meet Oshawa Foods' product needs in 2000, the juice business grew over the next decade to the point where we had to move it out of the snack plant to its own manufacturing facilities. With three plants in all, and multiple lines producing a variety of beverages, including juice, we were growing as a business and in market recognition.

I work in the juice business, and my brother, who started working with me in 2005, oversees the snack business. We separated the two companies in 2008, focusing on expanding each one—juice and snacks.

Under our beverage banner, I acquired two companies—one from Coke and the other from Power Packaging, giving us three facilities. I then consolidated all three into one in Etobicoke, where I can continue to grow that business from a single location.

Of course, regardless of whether we are making snacks or juice, our manufacturing plants in Mississauga (snacks) and Etobicoke (juice) are state of the art.

Two-Way Partnerships

Previously, I talked about the importance of partnerships and how Coke accommodated my request to scale back production for them for a brief period so that I could meet an urgent demand for Oshawa Foods. Although it was an unusual request, they were happy to accommodate me.

So, when they came to me with an unusual request for assistance, I was equally happy to accommodate them. As I said, partnerships are a two-way street.

For the Coca-Cola company, I was the first guy to bring the best and most innovative technology and processes to deliver diverse packaging at an affordable price. When Coke acquired two new product lines, they asked if we could train the new company's employees at our facility for two months, because we would show them how to effectively meet Coke's high standards for quality. There was one minor twist: the employees we were going to train worked for one of our competitors.

While the product they were manufacturing for Coke did not overlap with what we were making, they were still a competitor.

To most people on the outside looking in, agreeing to train our competitor's employees to elevate their capability to meet higher standards with a customer probably seems odd.

For clarification, acquiring our Calgary-based competitor enabled Coca-Cola to fill a need that did not conflict with our product offerings. Putting it more succinctly, it was not a product we made or planned to make in the future. However, because we had success in solving complex manufacturing processes, training these employees at our facilities would provide them with the needed expertise to solve a manufacturing problem for a segment of the business in which we were not involved. With that in mind and given our longstanding relationship with Coca-Cola, my view of the situation was that a partner of theirs is also a partner to us—especially since helping them would not put our company at a competitive disadvantage in the general marketplace.

Of course, if there were a potential issue or downside associated with their request, they would not have asked for my help. Let's face it, would Coca-Cola want us to work with one of their direct competitors, like Pepsi? The answer would be *no*, because our innovative insights provide Coke with a competitive advantage in the marketplace. They also respect and value the relationship with us as much as we value our relationship with them. Our symbiotic relationship is why they agreed to let us interrupt product delivery to meet Oshawa's short-term product demand and why we agreed to train a competitor's employees.

Some of you may still have a certain degree of skepticism, or perhaps some reservations about inviting a competitor into your business. Fair enough!

But here is the thing: the snack business is growing, and the juice business is growing. The good news is that what made me successful in every one of my ventures is the principles and the values I bring to what I am doing. And your principles and values will make your business successful, as these principles and values for success are universal, meaning it doesn't matter what business you are in; as long as you have the right mindset, success is accessible.

In the next chapter, we will talk about how success can be accessible to everyone.

About Those Friends

Earlier in this chapter, I mentioned that we all will need a little help from our friends every now and then. While having a great rapport with your customers is critical for your ongoing success—after all, people tend to deal with who they know, like, and trust, there is another group of equally important people.

I know you will say family, and you, of course, would be right. As I repeatedly stated throughout this book, I learned the values and the mindset for running a successful business from my father. He was also a great source of moral support. Sadly, this has not been the case in recent years, because of his mild dementia. As a side note, my success is an enduring part of his legacy, as my children's success will be a part of mine, which is another reason why family is so important. However, I am not talking about family here.

As is the case with anyone's life and business journey, I have had a few challenges and a few downturns over the years. During these times, I always went to my closest friends in my business forum and openly spoke about the issues I was facing. Beyond getting their moral support, I gained an outside-the-family perspective that led to new ideas and different ways of solving the problems I encountered.

People like Aubrey Dan immediately come to mind. Aubrey is a Canadian businessman and the son of Novopharm founder Leslie Dan. Besides being a philanthropist and a well-respected community member, he is, for me, a trusted friend.

Others in my circle include David Folk, Abe Glowinsky (president at The Incredible Clothing Company), Jeremy Freedman, Mark Gabourie (Timberland Equipment Limited), Chuck Philips, Michael Kalles (President, Harvey Kalles Real Estate

Limited), Sabine Viet (founder and CEO of Backerhaus Veit), Doug Irvine, and Geoff Hoy.

You may recognize some of these names (and their companies), some you may not. But I can tell you that these individuals have had and continue to have a positive impact on my life, as I hopefully have on theirs.

My point in sharing their names is to recognize their impact on my life and ask you who you have in your inner circle. Who can you go to in good times to celebrate, and in difficult times, to navigate?

While we should always strive for a high degree of self-sufficiency, John Donne's words, "no man [or woman] is an island" remind us that we do not take this journey alone in life—nor in business.

If you haven't yet, I would strongly encourage you to list the people in your personal forum whose input and friendship enrich your life as you enrich theirs.

CHAPTER 5:
Success Is Your Responsibility

I behave a certain way. It is not what happens around me that causes me to act a certain way, but my principles that drive my response. For example, in a previous chapter, I talked about the Pringles "can incident," in which the can manufacturer Sonoco backed out of their agreement to provide me with cans after they were pressured by P&G—another of their customers.

In short, their promise to me became expendable when a bigger customer—and a competitor of mine—threatened to pull their business. Their actions meant that external factors, which are not always in our control, drove their decision-making process, instead of their internal values. In a situation like this, what you can control is your response, which reflects your values and character.

While you can't count on things in the world always going your way, your character is a factor that is always under your control. You will ultimately come out the winner, as I did with the Pringles can incident, by recognizing this truth. Despite the eleventh-hour setback, I was able to find an alternative supplier that assured I got the required number of cans to produce the chips for Walmart and, in the process, increase my profitability.

In the meantime, the head of Sonoco (note, not *Sunoco*, which is one of the largest gas station/carwash franchise chains in Canada) lost more than my business and my respect. What he lost was far more valuable—his and the company's self-respect. While I cannot say that his specific decision to go back on his word with me directly impacted his employees or brand, I can't help but think that this is his pattern of behavior. If it is, I know that employees generally take a great deal of pride in the companies for whom they work, meaning that anything the company's leader does to tarnish its reputation will eventually impact employee morale and customer loyalty. Therefore, no amount of money can make up for the lost currency caused by a lost reputation. The decline may not be immediate or even apparent, but if that is the way you do business, it will inevitably come back to haunt you when you least expect it.

I am recounting the Sonoco story because it is intrinsic to the principle that your success is your responsibility.

Being the head of Sonoco, he chose a course of action—and maybe not for the first time—that will have a consequence.

In the meantime, I didn't allow the unfortunate circumstances of Sonoco's actions to cause panic or make me angry to the point that it derailed my entire project – which is probably the reaction they expected from me, given the significance of the deal with Walmart. As I have always done when confronted with a problem, I kept a cool head, which enabled me to rise to the challenge, find an alternative source for the cans, and increase my profit.

In this regard, your success is not determined by external circumstances alone.

Was this the only time I faced a difficult situation? Did my business vision and decisions always go as planned?

In the next chapter, I will share with you—in some detail—the most trying times I have ever faced as an entrepreneur and businessman, in which my measure of success was not in dollars and cents but in my ability to keep a cool head.

The remainder of this chapter will focus on the best way to view and overcome challenges.

Can I Do It?

Before taking on a challenge of either a new venture or a difficult situation, I ask myself if I can do it. If the answer is yes, then go for it. If you believe in it, you should stay the course and persevere. Like the famous Winston Churchill quote, when he emphatically states: "Never give in. Never give in. Never, never, never, never—in nothing, great or small, large, or petty—never give in, except to convictions of honour and good sense."

However, there is another side to his words that people often overlook.

While most people who are fervent believers in their vision usually cite the Churchill quote when they stubbornly stick with a plan in the face of impossible odds, they forget the last part of the saying. I am talking about the "never give in, except to convictions of honour *and* good sense."

Through this balanced lens, I assess my difficult times. I do this because when we think of successful people, we rarely look beyond their present-day success to see their journey and the setbacks they have overcome to get to where they are today.

I also share these insights with you to help you to realize that we all, in our journey, miss the mark and fall short of our expectations. However, setbacks and disappointments are not failures, because the only time you fail is when you compromise your values or ignore your good sense. In this regard, remaining true to who you are and what you value will keep you going—even if it means charting another course.

What Do You See through Your Lens?

Two shoe salespeople went to Africa—one came back and said no one was wearing shoes, so it must not be a good market, while the other came back excited, saying no one had shoes, so the market is wide open.

One saw the challenges and the likelihood of failure, while the other saw the opportunity and the possibility of success. Who was right? Your answer goes a long way toward predicting your reaction and outcome when encountering a challenge.

I like to think of it this way: with the first person, it is like coming up to the starting line of a race, and after seeing how many people are competing, you decide not to run because you believe you can't win.

With the second person, you see the field of competitors and are immediately energized by the possibility of winning the race.

The thinking with the latter is that while they may not win the race, at least they tried, and that is the key—to start—because you cannot tell by a high-level view or quick assessment of the field of runners whether you have a chance of winning.

But there is always a *but* to consider. What if you do some research before showing up at the starting line and discover that everyone in the race is an Olympic champion and world record holder? Do you expect to win? Should you still run?

The answer is obvious with my first runner: you don't quit the race before it starts based on an initial perception of the competition until after you have all of the facts. For that reason, almost everyone selects the second runner's choice – get enthusiastic and imagine yourself winning the race. In other words, give it a go because great things can happen if you try, while nothing will happen if you quit – right? The thing I find interesting is that no one stops to ask the question are you running the right race?

If you are an Olympic champion yourself, running against other champions makes sense because you bring something of equal or better skills to the starting line. If you are a weekend warrior runner and expect to win in a field of proven champions, you are more than likely to be disappointed with the results. Or, as the famous Sun Tzu quote from *The Art of War* advises, "Victorious warriors win first and then go to war, while defeated warriors go to war first and then seek to win."

Remember what I said about my commitment before entering a new market to always deliver a better-quality product at a better price? In a competitive field of champions, you must first win the race by knowing your competition and knowing if you can run faster and smarter. While backing down from a challenge before doing this assessment is surrender, meeting a challenge without proper evaluation will likely result in a similarly disappointing outcome. The only difference is that you end up wasting a lot of time and resources.

You must ask yourself, "Is my passion to win overshadowing my good judgement?"

A calculated passion or enthusiasm based on logic and an understanding of all the elements or factors you will face in your quest is the key to success. Know the opportunity for success and the potential downside for competing, decide if it is worth it, and then stick with it. This approach means an obstacle is either a challenge to endure and overcome, if warranted, or a meaningful warning sign to be respected.

Finding an Alternate Route to Success

Obstacles are inevitable, no matter what you do. Once you have decided on a course of action where you believe you can bring a better product or solution to the market at a more competitive price, you must be ready to face challenges and adapt quickly to respond to them.

With the Pringles chip cans, I found an alternate, better route to success by accepting and adapting to the reality that I was being hung out to dry by Sonoco. Instead of getting mad, I found a better way. The ability to adapt to unexpected changes, staying the course with a cool head, was the key to my successfully introducing a better alternative to a major brand's product offerings.

Deciding to move production from Canada to Mexico to serve a bigger, more profitable market for my microwave popcorn product is another example of taking an alternate route to achieve a successful outcome. In other words, I changed direction based on market demands versus rigidly adhering to the original plan of manufacturing the popcorn domestically.

Once again, the above examples demonstrate the importance of resiliency—not getting mad or frustrated when facing an obstacle but having the agility/adaptability to change course as circumstances warrant.

The Biggest Challenge You Will Face

Budding entrepreneurs often ask me about the biggest challenges they will face when they go into business.

If you have employees, earning the loyalty of the people with whom you work will be one of your biggest challenges. The key thing to remember is that people don't work for you when you own or manage a business; they work for themselves. They are an invaluable part of your success, for which they not only want to receive fair compensation but achieve a sense of accomplishment.

While compensation is important, money alone is not enough. Most people change jobs because they are not happy—this is especially true in this age of the great resignation or reshuffle. In short, people want to make a living, but they also want to be able to do something they love. Otherwise, they are punching a time clock and, in the process, are miserable.

I learned about the great resignation or reshuffling, as they call it, before it came into mainstream awareness, because of the COVID-19 pandemic.

I had an executive on my team who was exceptional at her job. While she was happy working with me and being part of the company, it was not her dream job. She told me that she was leaving the company to work in another industry one day. Obviously, I did not want to lose someone of this caliber, so the first thing I did was offer her more money. It turns out that money wasn't a primary factor in her decision to leave. She told me that she would actually be earning less money now by making the change. Think about that for a moment—someone taking a lower-paying job because they would be doing what they loved, and, as a result, getting a greater sense of accomplishment and happiness.

What was important was that I understood her reasons for wanting to move on, and even though I was disappointed to see her leave, I was happy for her and wished her well.

So, why do I say this will be one of the most difficult challenges you will face?

According to a March 2022 Harvard Business Review article, in the post-pandemic world, the transitory nature of employees is a significant problem, one with which "employers are likely to be contending with for years to come." The article's authors cite the "Five Rs: retirement, relocation, reconsideration, reshuffling, and reluctance" as the driving forces behind this trend.

What is most interesting is that this "new normal" transcends all industry sectors and involves all positions within an organization, from frontline workers to the executive suite.

Once again, money is still important, but people want something more. They are not afraid to actively pursue new opportunities to achieve a work-life balance, including a greater sense of purpose in what they do for a living. If you think about it and are honest about what you want to do and what you want to accomplish, you will see why people are starting to look beyond the paycheck. In this regard, the saying "if you do something you love, you will never have to work another day in your life" is truer now than ever before.

As a business owner and leader, I see my employees as more than a regular payroll to be met, but as partners with me on a shared journey. While we all have our specific tasks and must do them well, we all want the same thing—to be the best we can at what we do because we love doing it.

Of course, creating a positive working environment to sustain that passion is necessary. For example, we spent a great deal of money to create an employee space that was clean, safe, and highly functional—it was a good place to come to work every day.

We also invest in our employees through ongoing training and making them feel like they are a part of something special through our culture of communication and collaboration, with a clear purpose for what we all do as a collective company. Let's face it, the basic tasks associated with their jobs, they can do anywhere, with any manufacturer, in any industry. That is the reason why creating the right culture is so important. You don't want people who are just working for a paycheck, because if they are doing something they don't like or do not feel a sense of accomplishment in, they will ultimately leave or—even worse—stay for the wrong reasons and not bring their best to their jobs every day. In such a scenario, if many people work for you but wish they were doing something else, it eventually erodes company morale and the quality of the product or service you provide to the market.

In this context, while I never judge the decisions of another business executive, I can't help but wonder what Elon Musk thought when he sent an email to his extended management team. In the email in question, Musk told them that "they can work from home only after doing forty hours a week in the office" and that "employees who don't like the policy should depart Tesla."

How would you react if you were on the receiving end of an email like that from your boss?

Don't get me wrong; I support high standards of work ethic and performance. I have certain expectations from myself and my employees, from the factory floor to the c-suite. But I question how effective Elon Musk's blunt, heavy-handed approach will have in creating the right work atmosphere.

Other Challenges

There are, of course, other serious challenges we will all face over the coming months and years. For example, the breakdown or interruption of supply chains has far-reaching consequences that will reverberate throughout the entire world. Being in the snack food business, the very recent news of a pending popcorn shortage got my attention, as much as it will with moviegoers who can no longer buy what has always been a concession staple at theatres.

I also think that a potential proliferation of short-term, profit-driven carpetbaggers versus long-term business leaders could be another problem, with extended consequences for everyone. If you are in business or looking to start a business, how will you respond when facing a survival-of-the-fittest, predatory market?

While the above challenges may give you serious pause for concern, which they should, they will not ultimately determine your success. Your success reflects your personal values and responses to events that are not always in your control.

For me, my reason for being in business is to create a profitable and sustainable enterprise that produces a great product to serve the market better than anyone else, while generating a fair profit.

What is your reason for being in business?

Chapter 6:
Mindful Success

In the previous chapter, I talked about how your success is your responsibility. In other words, you can't be a spectator in your own journey—you must meet the challenges you will face head-on.

In this chapter, I want to talk about the obstacles you will face—not the types of challenges, but the way you respond to said challenges. In other words, how do you react when someone throws you a curveball? For example, what would you have done if you were me and faced the P&G situation regarding the Pringles can production issue?

Of course, it will be impossible for me to anticipate every external variable you will face in your journey. However, while I cannot offer specific advice tied to a particular situation, I can tell you what kind of mindset you need to bring to every problem in both success and failure.

Seeing Beyond Success

What do I mean when I say you have to "see beyond success"?

Often, when we look at someone who is successful, we only see the results of their ongoing journey. You will note that I used the term "ongoing journey." I will get to that in a moment.

The fact is that we do not see what went on before they arrived at success. In other words, our focus is on celebrating the outcome they achieved versus understanding (and celebrating) the ups and downs, wins and losses that led to where they are today. In this regard, we celebrate their achievements—which we should—but overlook the real secrets of their success, which comes through knowing and understanding their journey. Because their journey is continuing through and beyond their present success, the victory we witness today is not the exclamation point at the end of their story. It represents the building blocks on which they will continue to build even greater successes down the road. That is the continuing journey to which I referred earlier.

My Journey

In the late eighties, early nineties, non-alcoholic sparkling water was big. Made with 25 percent juice, the market went ballistic over the new product, and beverage manufacturers everywhere were getting into it. Convinced of the opportunity, I jumped into the market as well. Sadly, three to four years later, the market collapsed. There were two reasons this happened. First, it was a carbonated beverage, and was not as healthy of a drink as people initially thought. The second reason is that you could not drink a lot of it.

In three short years, production fell from thirty-eight million cases to five million, which taught me that you must differentiate between a fad product and a real business with long-term consumer demand. Even though I have stressed throughout this book that you have to offer a better product at a fair price to be profitable, the success of a particular product is ultimately determined by enough people wanting to buy enough of that product on an ongoing basis. Or, as someone once said to me, they bet that the last buggy whip manufacturer made the best product ever, but how many people need buggy whips today?

House Money
I had invested a significant amount of capital in equipment and building the line. It was a waste of money. My takeaway lesson: don't jump onto a fad bandwagon, but do your homework and find out what people think. Remember, you don't have to be the first in the market—only the best when entering it.

Even though my entry into the sparkling water business was not subject to my usual due diligence, my rule of never investing what you cannot afford to lose served me well. I am not saying that I had an easy-come, easy-go attitude regarding my financial loss. I am saying that based on the success of my existing businesses, I was playing with house money. And while nobody likes losses, there is a world of difference between not wanting to lose and not being able to afford to lose. With the former, you can afford to learn your lessons and move on—which I did, e.g., I could exit the sparkling water market intact with only a slight buffeting of my pride. The lessons you learn are of little comfort when you have to throw in the towel and are out of business.

Not everything I have done was a success. Periodic failures are a necessary part of your success journey. Just make sure that you can continue that journey.

A Fading Picture
There are two potential downsides or traps to avoid when it comes to success.

In the first instance, success can create a sense of complacency and risk aversion. I will share the Kodak story with you momentarily.

In the second instance, being successful can create a high level of confidence bordering on arrogance. Because you are a proven winner, you may feel that you can take it easy or take shortcuts and still end up on top. Like the saying about all roads leading to Rome, in both cases, the roads here lead to failure.

Let's look at Kodak as an example of complacency and risk aversion.

Talk about becoming a victim of your past success. For many years, the Rochester-based icon enjoyed steady and sure profits from its traditional film business. Not only did this create a sense of security, but it also caused the company to ignore the internal voices of key personnel sounding the alarm of pending change.

In Kodak's case, the pending change came in the form of digital technology. That's right: the company's good fortune was washed away by the tide of discontinuous innovation and the growing market awareness of the negative ecological impact of the manufacturing process associated with its mainstay product offerings.

What few people realize is that, as was the case in 1889, when Kodak introduced the first camera, the company was actually the first to develop the digital imaging technology with which we are all familiar today. That's right: before the emergence of other players in the market, Kodak was way ahead of its time and poised to take commanding control of the digital market opportunity through a strategic conversion of its loyal, global customer base.

Unfortunately, rather than seeing the digital age as an opportunity to continue its dominance as a market leader, the company's leadership saw it as a threat to its existing line of traditional film products. As a result, and much to the disappointment of the executive team in their digital division, Kodak relegated the new technology to a permanent holding pattern. This decision opened the door to its competition. In January 2012, with $6.75 billion in liabilities against just $5.1 billion in assets, the company that had been in existence for 123 years had to declare bankruptcy.

Of course, in some cases, overconfidence (arrogance) can be as lethal to a business as complacency.

Too Big To Fail

If you read the book or saw the movie based on Andrew Ross Sorkin's *Too Big to Fail: The Inside Story of How Wall Street and Washington Fought to Save the Financial System – and Themselves*, you will know what I mean when I talk about pride coming before the fall.

I will leave it to you to either read the book or watch the movie to learn the specific details of the 2008 mortgage industry crisis. However, as the title implies, driven by greed and believing in their own invincibility, financial institutions abandoned good business practices, making loans that exposed them and, ultimately, the country and the world to a potentially catastrophic economic collapse.

Were they really too big to fail? No, but they were too big for the government to stand by and do nothing. At a whopping cost of $498 billion to taxpayers, the government bailed out global giants such as Citigroup, Bank of America, JPMorgan, Wells Fargo, and AIG.

It is safe to say that for most businesses, a similar government bailout is not likely on the table for any reason, let alone poor business practices.

Finding the Success Balance

Finding the right "success" balance between complacency and confidence is critical. Put another way, you need a reliable compass to guide you. For me, and I think for everyone, it is always finding the best way to serve the market's needs with integrity.

Suppose your decisions are driven by delivering the best product or service at a fair price while making a reasonable profit. In that case, you can successfully navigate any situation and come out on top.

Also, accept the fact that you will encounter setbacks and hardships in your journey. The important thing to remember is that you must always stay calm and keep your emotions in check—which is easier said than done.

For example, when Sonoco pulled the proverbial rug out from under me when they said they would not supply me with the promised Pringles-type chip cans to fulfill my Walmart orders, my first reaction was to deal with the problem. Don't get me wrong; I was both disappointed and mad. However, I flipped a switch, stayed calm, and found the solution by never losing sight of the bigger picture: serving the consumer's best interests.

That said, when the dust had settled, and I dealt with the crisis successfully, when Sonoco called me afterwards, I told them in no uncertain terms that I would never forget what they had done.

Always Focus on the Future
Don't dwell on past events, because you can't change them. It's done. Keeping your focus on the future, where your success lies.

No matter where you are in your business journey today or your challenges, you can apply the above lessons and chart a new and better course. It is never too late! Before setting up my original lines, I secured several large contracts. With the contracts in hand, I then invested in the lines to fulfill my contractual obligations. My investment in the new lines was significant, but I felt good because I had done my due diligence and had firm commitments—or so I thought.

Through circumstances beyond my control, the clients cancelled several orders. With the new lines in place, I was all dressed up with nowhere to go.

I want to emphasize this was not the only time circumstances threw me a curveball. When you have been doing business as long as I have, there will be many times that you will have to deal with the unexpected.

While each challenge was different, the one constant was my willingness to look to the future with equal amounts of calm determination, confidence, and optimism.

In the case of the above contract cancellations, I won new and richer contracts than the original ones I had lost. Like the saying that chance favours the prepared mind, by staying calm, I was able to look beyond the circumstances to realize an even better opportunity.

Staying calm in difficult situations is one thing. Staying calm when dealing with difficult people is another matter. I will discuss this topic in the next chapter.

Chapter 7:
It's Not Personal?

I t isn't personal; it's just business.

We have all heard this timeless saying at one point or another in our daily lives, but is it really true?

Let's start with a personal, true story regarding my dealings with Canadian grocery store magnate Steve Stavro's company, Knob Hill Farms.

I was young and had just started the business, and had scheduled a meeting for first thing in the morning with the Stavro team. I sat in the waiting room for hours beyond the scheduled meeting time—until 10:00 or 10:30. Despite the frustration, I was able to land the business and was told to come back tomorrow to pick up the order. The same thing happened the next day. I showed up for our 7:30 a.m. meeting on time, and again, had to wait a couple of hours before getting in.

Funny thing . . . I noticed that they had a big lounge, with a snooker table and a food buffet, and from what I could tell, the sales guys spent all their time relaxing. I wondered who was looking after their suppliers and customers. Let's say it did not leave me with a good impression.

When I finally returned to my office with the promised order in hand, I told my dad what had happened. I told him how I had had to wait again and what I had seen in the lounge. My dad told me there was a right way and a wrong way to do business. If we do business, we need to do it honorably and with respect. He told me, "These guys are not respecting you." We fulfilled this first order as promised and did not take any further orders from them.

We did not sell to them from that day on. Even though they called me regularly to place an order, we said sorry, we do not supply you—and we didn't supply them for eleven years.

Why would we walk away from business with a large food chain?

Keeping me waiting not once, but twice, told me they didn't respect my time. It was downright dismissive, bordering on arrogance.

I decided by their actions, that they didn't respect suppliers, so we were not going to work with them. After all, we had a standard for doing business: mutual respect. And no amount of money will replace it.

The Real Thing

Coca-Cola has been a long-term partner, but the road with that relationship was not always smooth. For example, about two years ago, I called their VP, asking to meet with them about our pricing. With rising costs, I needed to revisit our arrangement. When he somewhat dismissively asked me why I wanted to meet with him, I told him we needed to talk about our pricing. He said, "And if we don't do anything about the pricing, what will happen?" I told him that as of tomorrow, we would no longer work with them.

Think about it for a moment: a giant, multinational global company that had a twenty-million-dollar contract with us was unwilling to meet with me to even talk about a price adjustment. My only reasonable response was to tell him that I was prepared to walk away. My reasoning was that true respect between partners is when they listen and talk to one another to reach a mutually rewarding outcome. If you don't have that, then you are little more than a transaction on a balance sheet—easily replaced.

Remember what I have been saying throughout this book: you must strive to offer a better product at a fair price than what is currently available. In other words, offer your customers better value than they can get anywhere else. That said, your premium value has a cost in more than just dollars—it is called mutual respect.

When I called the VP from Coca-Cola to discuss the need to revisit our pricing arrangement, he should have said, thank you for reaching out to me, let's get together because you are a valued partner. But, instead of saying, "I want to understand the challenges you are facing to see how we can work together to address them," he questioned why we should meet at all. He didn't even want to talk about it.

Remember, doing business is a two-way street, upon which each partner's contribution must be mutually rewarding and beneficial beyond a financial transaction. If you a partner with no partnership, then you shouldn't be working with the other party.

This belief is not only the epitome of respect but a reflection of the shared values that produce the right outcome: mutual success.

Another important lesson here is that your view of money and the perceived power it brings is a potential trap that can undermine your business, relationships, and ultimate success.

Steve Stavro's company thought that because they would be a large account for me, they could always show up hours late for a meeting. Conversely, the Coca-Cola VP may have thought they didn't have to revisit pricing because they were a big company and I would simply accept it.

How many business owners would accept this kind of treatment or do business with someone who did not respect the relationship as much as they should? I am not only talking about their respecting you, but you having respect for yourself. Self-respect is the great equalizer in any business dealings, and having self-respect is *personal*—which is why business is personal.

What happened with Coca-Cola?

The president heard about my call with the VP and went crazy. I received a call back asking what happened, and I told them. The VP then called me back and asked if I would meet with him for coffee. When we met, he apologized for how he had treated me and how dismissive he had been regarding my price concerns. We are still doing business to this day, successfully navigating the challenges we both faced during the pandemic.

Creating the Right "Personal" Culture

In recent years, there has been increasing talk about the importance of creating the right culture within your company. In other words, the level or quality of service attitude you find on the frontlines of an organization, be it sales or support, originates at the top.

Respect begins with the leadership of the company. Over my entire career, there were only two times that leaders attempted to influence me by flexing their muscles in their dealings with me.

What did I do when that happened, or when it happens today?

In today's highly transactional, virtually connected world, my principles of mutual respect may seem quaint or outdated. Many would argue that "might is right" and that being successful in business requires a *you-don't-get-what-you-deserve, you-get-what-you-negotiate*, winner-take-all mindset.

I certainly would not argue the point that, with all that has happened, the mounting pressures threatening a business's survival are more of a concern now than ever before. As a result, talking about respect and having the courage to walk away from business if it is lacking may seem outdated or out of touch. But bad business is still bad business, and if you deal with someone you can't trust or with someone who is only in it for themselves, it will catch up with you and end up costing you more than you could ever get from such a relationship. When I talk about cost, I am also talking about self-respect.

Business is personal because the attitude you bring to a relationship reflects your personal views and values, whether you serve a client or a customer. In short, who you are in business is who you are in everyday life. It is your personal brand, both with your customers and those with whom you work. And it is those personal values that enable you as a business leader to establish the right culture within your organization, whether you are a sole proprietor or the head of a major corporation with thousands of workers.

The Either/Or Myth

I think it is important to pause here and reflect on what I said in the previous section.

I want to stress that, sadly, not everybody thinks this way. I have encountered many people who believe that being a straight shooter and treating others with respect compromises success rather than building it. You know the saying about nice guys finishing last.

I want to stress right now that having integrity and working with someone to achieve a mutual gain doesn't mean allowing people to take advantage of you. If you are in a business relationship like that now, get out and look for better and brighter opportunities. Seek out business partners who share the same values with you in deeds as much as in their words.

It doesn't mean that you will always agree or not have difficult conversations from time to time. But with a good partner, you can have the transparency and honesty to work through any situation to everyone's benefit. Remember, this is not a zero-sum game, where there has to be a winner and a loser.

Look back to an earlier chapter in this book and how I agreed to train the employees of a competitor to enable them to produce a new product for Coca-Cola. Your initial reaction might have been, "What was he thinking?" Why help a competitor? As I indicated in that chapter, it was for a product I didn't provide, demonstrating to Coca-Cola that I valued our partnership.

In turn, they showed me how much they valued me as a partner when they apologized for not initially responding in the right way to my request to review pricing. They didn't come back to me because I was bigger and stronger or had leverage over them. They came back because they knew they could trust me and that I would always do a great job for them, even when it meant helping a competitor address a need I didn't provide.

It's a People Thing

You may wonder why I spend so much time discussing personal values and relationships in a business book. It's because everything involved in a business is personal, because it involves people and the values and principles they bring to the workplace every day.

My company's success starts within me as a business leader. My values and success mindset filter through to my employees— doing what I do in a given situation always aligns with what I say and the values I champion. Is there a consistency in my actions that creates certainty and confidence with the people with whom I share this journey, starting with my employees and ultimately extending to our customers?

In the above context, business is personal, and it is about people.

For example, I will not take advantage of a situation at someone else's expense and then justify it by saying it's just business; it *is* personal, because what you do reflects who you are as a person. More importantly, what you do impacts others and influences their reaction to you and your words. More importantly, what you do impacts others and influences their reaction to you and your words. Knowing and caring that you have an impact on someone else not only gives them a better understanding of who you are but also builds trust. It also allows you to understand them better and make more insightful decisions regarding your dealings with them.

For example, what message did the head of the company that hung me out to dry with the Pringles-type packaging send to not only me, but to his employees?

The answer is obvious: I couldn't trust him. And being unable to trust someone is about as personal as you can get. However (and this is probably something he didn't consider), what message did he send to his employees who had been dealing with me? Is having integrity based on the situation or convenience? If he were to do that to a good client (which I was), then what would he do to a good employee if, in his mind, the situation warranted it? Employees aren't just a number on your payroll ledger; they are people, and what they see and think about what you do is personal.

In this context, there is no on/off switch when it comes to integrity. Nor is there an opaque partition separating you and your actions as a businessperson from you, the person. Who you are at night when you are at home is ultimately who you are when you are at the office and vice versa.

When I walked away from doing business with Steve Stavro's company, I did it for personal reasons (and values).

When I told Coca-Cola I would stop doing business with them, I did it for personal reasons (and values).

You can't separate the personal and business.

So, what does this have to do with dealing with difficult people?

In the end, the best way to deal with difficult people—in fact, all people—is to be true to yourself and the values you have as a person, whether you are at home or in the office.

Business is *personal!*

Chapter 8:
Integrity, Commitment, Perseverance

We all have a sense of purpose that is unique to us and drives us to achieve whatever it is we value most.

As discussed in the previous chapter, no one can (or should) dictate your motivations for doing something, because you are playing to your strengths or ideals. In short, your integrity, purpose, and commitment to whatever you say and do are ultimately up to you. Of course, staying true to oneself does not always pave an easy road—but no one said life would always be easy or fair. That's why circumstantial loyalty to yourself—to who you are and what you believe—is the fastest way to be led astray.

Now, I want to caution you that fervently believing in something does not mean that you abandon good advice or positive critiquing from a reliable and trusted source. I place particular emphasis on the words *reliable* and *trusted*. Maintaining objectivity is critical in difficult, heat-of-the-moment battles. Trusted advisors are important because they offer you—or should offer you—an outside-the-box, broader-lens view of a situation. It is up to you if you change course or stay on the path you are already going. The key is to choose the right advisors—ones who will, when the situation requires it, challenge your thinking versus giving sycophantic support to your every thought. Or, as a senior executive once said, if both of us agree on everything all the time, then one of us is redundant. Another way to say it is that being true to yourself does not mean you are above being challenged, either by yourself or someone close to you. Any idea or thought that is good, honest, and right can take the heat of questioning and enable you to accept scrutiny confidently and calmly.

Within this framework, let's now examine what integrity of actions, a commitment of purpose, and perseverance of values look like through my personal journey and experiences.

Walking My Talk

Whenever someone offers advice, I immediately think of a phrase from the book *Table Talk* by John Seldon. The book, written in 1654 and published after his death in 1689, is the first time the saying "do as I say, and not as I do" was used. Its meaning is obvious, and its intent is a call to challenge any advice you receive based on whether the person providing it lives by it. In other words, are they doing the thing they are telling you to do and having success with it? If not, why would you listen to them?

In each of the examples or stories I will share with you in the final few pages of this book, there will be one common theme on which you can count. When it comes to the integrity of actions, the commitment of purpose, and the perseverance of values, I walk my talk. It doesn't mean you have to do things exactly how I do them. What it means is that the core principles of what I base my life on—integrity, commitment, and perseverance—should serve as your guide on the different roads that your life and business journey will inevitably take. After all, and I think I said this earlier, all roads, though different, lead to Rome—and all success is based on these three core principles.

CHAPTER 9:
Integrity Of Actions

in·teg·ri·ty /in'tegrədē/ - the quality of being honest
and having strong moral principles; moral uprightness.
"He is known to be a man of integrity."

W hat is integrity? Sure, it means being honest and telling the truth, but it is more than the spoken word. Integrity is not only what you say but backing it up by what you do—especially during difficult or challenging times.

For example, earlier in this book, I told you about how a company with whom I had been dealing hung me out to dry by backing out of their commitment to providing me with cans for my no-name version of Pringles potato chips. Was I disappointed? Yes! Was I angry? Yes—but controlled. For me, exacting revenge or making them pay was not a priority. Honouring my commitment to my customer was the priority. This commitment enabled me to shift focus to taking productive actions that inevitably returned a greater reward, both professionally and personally.

Do not get me wrong here—I will not forget what the company did to me and how the vice president of sales responded with dismissive arrogance. But my revenge came from my ability to turn their actions into a positive, versus stooping to their level. That's right, I am a "powerful little guy"—but not because of any underhanded, nefarious response in kind, but because my focus was on serving my customer's needs versus exacting my pound of flesh from someone with whom I will never deal again. And that, my friend, is the second part of my revenge. Besides turning a bigger profit than I would have had he kept his word, he lost the opportunity to work with someone who would always be straightforward and make him money.

This example is what I mean by one having integrity of action.

One of the many reasons I am writing this book is not to put my accomplishments center stage, but to help many people find their own version of the success I have enjoyed.

Over the past five years, many new companies have talked to me about building a successful business. From entrepreneurs to young students in their twenties and thirties, people are looking for a direction—a path that they can follow that aligns with their goals and unique skills or gifts.

So, realistically, when I talk about having an integrity of action, it isn't just how I govern myself. It is also the legacy and impact I make by introducing these principles of enduring success to as many people as possible. Think of me as a caretaker of these principles, which my family has followed over the past seven hundred years. By applying them to how you live and work, you are not following me but working toward your true inner potential and the great things you can achieve.

The integrity of action never loses sight of this bigger picture: enabling your customers, partners, and friends to realize their goals and dreams.

CHAPTER 10:
Commitment Of Purpose

pur·pose /ˈpərpəs/ – *the reason for which something is done or created or for which something exists. "The purpose of the meeting is to appoint a trustee."*

Why do you do what you do?

From the loftiness of philosophical debate to the everyday reality of working to pay the bills, there must be more than a reason for what you do—there has to be a purpose. It doesn't have to be a grand vision of becoming a global icon of success or an altruistic champion of change—though you will very likely change your world and everyone in it through what you do.

What I am talking about is the difference between purpose and reason. Purpose is *why* you do something—your ultimate end goal—while *reason* is how you do the things you do to achieve that purpose.

What is the reason you go to work to earn a living? To provide a better life for your family—this is the purpose.

Why did I get into the patio furniture business or, for that matter, the beverage and snack business? While my reasons and the circumstances were different in each situation, my ultimate purpose was to deliver a high-quality product at a fair price, on time—all of the time. Whether it's rattan, popcorn, or beverages, my purpose is to do it better than anyone else in my industry. That is the reason I would come in early or stay late to learn everything there was to learn about the product I was making, regardless of what that product was.

In this context, reason and purpose are two very different but related things. But having a reason to do something without having a sincere purpose will not take you anywhere in life.

Going back to my earlier example about working to pay the bills, how many people do it without a purpose—or, worse yet, a *meaningful* purpose? How many out there are punching the clock and counting down the days to their retirement? How many people are working to pay off a mortgage or debt but doing something they don't love, that isn't fulfilling, or that does not take full advantage of their talents?

In his famous quote, Albert Pike said, "What we do for ourselves dies with us. What we do for others and the world remains and is immortal." Talk about having a purpose! Unfortunately, we usually think that purpose or having a purpose has to be on a *grand scale*. Nothing could be further from the truth.

What determines the real impact and depth of your purpose is really knowing the reason why you do something and the motivation that drives you to be the best at it. It is what causes you to go that extra mile, beyond the minimum job requirements, where you can see the impact of what you do beyond the action itself. I guess I am saying that having a reason to do something is not enough unless you can tie it to a more meaningful purpose. Without this purpose, very few will achieve their true potential.

Now, these may sound like intangible, even fanciful musings. Fair enough. But why do you think we are experiencing the great resignation in the post-pandemic world?

Searching for a Greater Purpose

According to a recent *Forbes* article, people are voluntarily leaving their current jobs in record numbers. While this trend began before the pandemic, the crisis seems to have accelerated people's motivation to seek something better.

While the "desire for greater financial security" is a factor behind so many people "rethinking their entire career paths," something is happening at a deeper level. It turns out that "individuals are evaluating what is important and fulfilling to them."

Remember I told you the story about an executive on my team who was exceptional at her job? Even though she was happy working with me and being part of the company, it was not her dream job. When she told me she was leaving, the first thing I did was offer her more money. She turned me down, telling me that she was actually going to be making less money than she was in her current position.

That is the true definition of knowing and having purpose. While my executive's reason for working was to make money to pay the bills, ultimately, her purpose was tied to something more than the size of her paycheck.

Borrowing the line from the old MasterCard commercials, *knowing your purpose is priceless.*

Do you know your purpose?

CHAPTER 11:
Perseverance Of Values

val·ue /ˈvalyōo/ - *a person's principles or standards of
behavior; one's judgment of what is important in life.*
"They internalize their parents' rules and values."

You must have values to provide value.

The industry I am in knows me. People see that I am open and transparent in my dealings with them. There is an element of trust when you are not only delivering *value* in your product but *values* in how you do business.

For example, helping a competitor provide my client Coca-Cola with a product line I was not set up to do spoke to the values I brought to the relationship. Suppose my values were tied solely to protecting my turf and feeling threatened by a competitor dealing with a good client. In that case, I may not have agreed to train their employees to ramp up their capability to deliver their best product.

For some, this level of openness and cooperation is the antithesis of how to do business in a *you-don't-get-what-you-deserve, but-what-you-negotiate* world. As you read the previous paragraph, you might have wondered, *What was Yahya thinking?!*

That is a fair question. But here is the thing: what did *Coca-Cola* think?

Let's say a worst-case scenario occurs—such as when my competitor, after getting in the door, decided to try and poach business from me. With whom do you think a reputable company like Coca-Cola would prefer to deal? What impact would such a move have on their relationship with Coca-Cola? If you were Coca-Cola, would you be inclined to deal with someone who tried to back-door your trusted partner after said partner helped to bring them up to speed?

I am not naïve. I am sure there are some companies who, in the client's position, might entertain such advances by a competitor if they could see a better deal on the table. However, remembering our core purpose to always deliver a high-quality product at a fair price, on time, all of the time makes us hard to beat. This commitment, plus the openness and loyalty we bring to our business relationships, means we will never have a justifiable reason to compromise our values for any supposed short-term gain. It also means that our clients won't.

When all is said and done, the integrity of your actions, commitment to your purpose, and unyielding perseverance in your values make you a formidable competitor.